I Know That Tune!

Written by Diana Noonan • Illustrated by Fraser Williamson

Grandpa gave Katy a recorder
for her birthday.
She took it outside
and she played a tune.

Dad heard the tune.
He said, "I know that tune. I do, I do!"
So he picked up his trumpet
and he played the tune too.

Grandma heard the tune.
She said, "I know that tune. I do, I do!"
So she picked up her flute
and she played the tune too.

The truck driver heard the tune.
She said, "I know that tune. I do, I do!"
So she picked up her guitar
and she played the tune too.

The shopkeeper heard the tune.
He said, "I know that tune. I do, I do!"
So he picked up his violin
and he played the tune too.

The rubbish collector heard the tune.
He said, "I know that tune. I do, I do!"
So he picked up his banjo
and he played the tune too.

"We know that tune," they said.
"We do, we do!"
So they all played the tune.

Twinkle, twinkle little star,
How I wonder what you are,
Up above the world so high,
Like a diamond in the sky.
Twinkle, twinkle little star,
How I wonder what you are!